THE SECRET OF COOKING FOR DOGS

MARTIN A. GARDNER

The Secret of
Cooking for Dogs

Illustrated by Clare Barnes, Jr.

DOUBLEDAY & COMPANY, INC.

GARDEN CITY, NEW YORK

1964

I am deeply indebted to a number of people who helped a great deal in the preparation of this book.

I am happy to express deepest gratitude to Dr. James R. Kinney, who has been practicing for many years, over thirty of them at Ellin Prince Speyer Hospital in New York City where he was chief veterinarian and director. He is also chief veterinarian of the Westminster Kennel Club at Madison Square Garden in New York City. Dr. Kinney gave generously of time, effort, knowledge, and professional advice, and his suggestions were most helpful.

Mr. Thomas Baldino and his charming wife, Catherine, have assisted me in many ways in solving some of the textual problems.

Dr. Leonard Greenfield, of Maplewood, New Jersey, a practicing "people" doctor for many years, was a great help in the nutritional aspects of preparing this book.

Many thanks to the library staff at the American Kennel Club, in New York City, for allowing me to investigate their vast resources.

Also thanks to the kind staff at the Gaines Dog Research Center for giving me free rein in their library.

The public relations departments of the various commercial dog food companies deserve thanks for generously providing me with pamphlets and other printed material that were full of valuable information.

Finally, my appreciation to the many anonymous dog owners, from bustling Park Avenue street corners to rambling Virginia lawns, who contributed much information and help in preparing the recipes in this book.

MARTIN A. GARDNER
New York City
June 1963

Preliminary study of sheep dog eating

Final sketch of sheep dog eating

CONTENTS

Spirited study of sheep dog in motion

Study of English sheep dog resting

THE SECRET OF COOKING FOR DOGS

Study of head, side view

Attention, Fellow Dog Lovers . . .

This is a cookbook for your dog. Why? Well, the most important factor in maintaining your dog's good health is the way in which you feed him. Your dog cannot select his own dinner, he'll eat only what you give him, so *you* have to make sure that he's getting the best possible nourishment.

You see, dogs are a little like children. If a dog could be left to choose meals for himself, he'd be more than likely to select food that appeals to his taste rather than his well-being. Therefore, the essence of good meal planning for your dog is simply this: *He'll be better off eating small amounts of the proper food than great quantities of table scraps or slop.*

As you know, your dog is a carnivore—a meat eater. (This doesn't mean that he should exist on just meat—he should eat some starches and fats, too.) No matter how much you love him, though, you don't have to feed him sirloin steak! He'll be perfectly happy with the cheaper cuts of meat, even horse meat. In addition to the emphasis on meat, he should eat some vegetables, starches, cheese, milk, and eggs, to give him some of the elements he needs for his health and well-being. Included in this cookbook are recipes that utilize all of these essential foods for your dog.

The dog is a carnivore

But how often and how much do you feed your dog? For the average dog (not the toy breeds or giant breeds), from weaning to three months feed him four times a day, for three months to six months three times a day, from six months to one year twice a day, and after one year just once a day. The amount to feed him depends on the breed, age, weight, and condition of the animal. Another factor is his habitat. Obviously, the city dog will require less to eat than the country dog, since the city dog usually gets less exercise. The recipes in this book are geared for small- or medium-sized dogs. You may have to adjust the amounts of food for your own pet. Perhaps you'll want to check with your veterinarian to make sure how much he should eat.

And, by the way, your veterinarian is the best authority on the proper care and feeding of your dog. The veterinarian is a completely trained doctor who is dedicated to animals. Make sure that you take your dog to the same doctor every time, so that he can get to know your pet. And, just as important, take your dog to the veterinarian, not only when there is an emergency, but for regular checkups. Remember: *Don't be afraid to consult your veterinarian at any time.* He is primarily concerned with your dog's health, just as your own doctor is concerned with your health.

City dogs get less exercise

A final word: You should not be too concerned about the way you prepare dinner for your dog. He may like you to give him a steady diet of canned food, or he may like you to cook for him.

If he likes commercial pet food for every meal, give it to him. The commercial pet food is good. The pet-food manufacturers have a perfectly balanced diet in their foods which will completely satisfy the needs of your dog. The manufacturers spend thousands of dollars in research in order to improve their products so that your dog can get the food that will be best for him.

But, if your dog prefers that you augment the prepared pet foods with your own cooking, or if you intend to cook all of his meals, this book is for you.

The sound of pots and pans . . .

The information and recipes that follow are intended to serve only as guides. They are not the final word on meal making for your pet. For the most part, the recipes are quick and easy to prepare.

Every dog owner develops his own theories about the feeding of his animal. With this in mind, dear dog owner, we hope that you enjoy this cookbook for dogs, and that you find it answers some of the questions you would like to ask about your pet. Happy cooking!

1
Meat: The Champion!

So you're going to cook dinner for your dog!

So you're going to cook dinner for your dog! Well, it doesn't take an expert to know that his basic food is meat. Dogs are carnivores. Even if he is a follower of George Bernard Shaw and introduces himself as the last of the canine vegetarians, don't you believe it. Any resemblance between your dog and G. B. Shaw is purely skin deep. Yes, meat is the champion when it comes to feeding your dog. Why, this is such a well-known fact that in a grocery store near my home there is a little slogan over the meat counter which reads, "Man is dog's best friend . . . especially if that man is Max, your friendly butcher."

Preparing meat for your dog is really simple. Among the more demonstrative of the canine debaters, however, there are violently barked arguments about the pros and cons of cooked vs. raw meat as a main course.

Any resemblance to G. B. Shaw is purely skin deep

Some dogs won't eat anything but raw meat. On the other hand, others look down their snouts at the raw stuff and prefer slightly browned, if not downright well-done, victuals.

Naturally, there are advantages and disadvantages to both sides of the argument. One school of culinary thought contends that the cooking of meat for dogs destroys some of its mineral and vitamin content. This is true. Raw meat is the best single source of minerals and vitamins for our four-legged friends. Of course, the way to minimize this loss of minerals and vitamins is to save the juices and gravies that flow from the cooked meat, and include them in the dog's dinner.

The other culinary camp argues that cooked meat is much more vital for dogs because of its flavor value. The flavor and odor of meat are enhanced when it is cooked, and thus the dog's digestive juices start flowing before he begins to gnaw away. This is highly desirable in making for a healthy, happy hound.

Most dogs agree that it really doesn't matter if their meat is cooked or raw. If your dog prefers cooked meat, he is truly the refined urbanite! And, if this *is* the case, you should mix some vegetables in with the meat. This enables your dog to get his laxatives right in his dinner! You see, before the dog became sophisticated, that is, during his survival-of-the-fittest stage, he was a wild,wolf-like animal. He hunted and ate game, not stopping to differentiate flesh, innards, and skin. The skin, hair, and innards of the wild dog's prey served as the natural laxative his system needed. But now, with your dog being so citified and selective in his choice of food, you must make the compensation for the lack of laxative in his diet by adding roughage, or vegetables, to his meals. Of course, no matter how urban your dog is, he should get an occasional dinner of raw meat so that he doesn't forget his heritage and birthright.

And here's more food for thought! If your dog has been putting on weight lately, and is beginning to resemble an overstuffed sausage, put him on an all-meat diet. Meat will never fatten a dog, no matter how much of it he gulps down. Meat will keep him tip-top without giving him a flip-flop shape!

Is your dog a lazy lout, just sitting around the house keeping the carpet warm? Or is he an active worker? Well, if he is a K-9 to 5 type, feed him all the meat you can afford. Meat is primarily a food for active dogs. Some dog owners I know insist that a diet composed of 50 per cent meat for the working dog is just the right amount to keep him punching the time clock. But, if you have an executive dog, meat can have its drawbacks. Since meat is so concentrated a food, it may not set too well with the Executive Setter during his attacks of acid indigestion!

In general, however, you can never give too much meat to your dog. Human beings can eat only so much meat, then our bodies be-

Originally your dog was a wild, wolf-like animal

St. Bernard before *a good dinner . . .*

gin to reject it. This is why we "grow tired" of meat eating. But dogs are never harmed by meat as humans are. A dog will eat all the meat he can get his paws on!

And the best favor you can grant him is to give him a variety of meat meals. Dogs can eat just about any kind of meat (except pork). It will not harm your dog if you feed him beef, lamb, bacon, chicken, kidney, heart, liver, or tripe.

Here are a few things to remember when you cook meat for your dog. The muscle meat (breast meat) is the most easily digested. He will have a little trouble with the long-fibered meats, such as leg parts. And, dogs go wild over the glandular organs, such as liver, kidney, heart, and tripe. These, by the way, are the most inexpensive meats you can purchase from your pal Max, the butcher. Chances are, if you get friendly with your butcher, he'll give you a cut rate on some of these inexpensive, and highly nourishing, innards. The important thing to remember is that innards spoil much more rapidly than does muscle meat. Therefore, serve them soon after purchasing. It is better to give your dog no meat at all than meat that is no good at all!

And since we've gotten down to the meat of the subject, let's look a little more closely at bones. Bones are your dog's toy and his toothbrush. When he gnaws on a bone he helps himself to keep his

St. Bernard after a good dinner . . .

teeth strong and active. Also, bones will help in reducing the tartar on his teeth. Most dog owners agree that just soft knucklebones should be fed to dogs because they won't splinter and they're harmless. Almost any kind of bone is edible (except fish- and fowl bones), but you should be especially careful of steak and chops, since they tend to splinter. The great amount of hydrochloric acid in a dog's stomach should readily attack any fragments of bone he may swallow, minimizing the danger of stabbing himself in the stomach.

So remember, you may be the greatest cook in the world, or just another can't-boil-water type, but the simplest and best food for your dog is an elegant meal of meat. Meat is truly the champion!

I.M.L. (Instant Meat Loaf)

> ¼ *pound ground meat*
> ½ *small onion, diced*
> ⅛ *teaspoon salt*
> ¼ *cup fresh bread crumbs*
> ½ *can condensed vegetable soup, undiluted*
> *Handful of dog biscuits*

Mix meat with other ingredients. Bake in oven 15 minutes or until done. Add biscuits. Serve warm.

The bone is a dog's toothbrush

MEAT SURPRISE

¼ *pound chopped meat*
1 *small carrot, sliced*
1 *small onion, sliced*
⅛ *cup diced celery*
Garlic powder
Salt
Tomato purée

Cover bottom of pot with water. Cook carrot, onion, and celery until tender. Add chopped meat and season. Cook until meat is brown on outside. Add some purée and cook about 5 minutes. Serve warm.

RICE AND SHINE!

½ can meat balls in gravy for dogs
1 small onion, chopped
½ green pepper, diced
1 small can tomatoes, drained
Margarine
¼ cup instant rice
⅛ teaspoon salt

Cook meat balls as directed on can. Sauté onion, pepper, and tomatoes in margarine, stirring frequently. Add seasoned, cooked instant rice. Add meat balls. Serve warm.

MEAT-LOAF LEFTOVERS

1 cup leftover meat loaf
½ cup cottage cheese
Leftover vegetables

Combine meat loaf, cheese, and warmed vegetables. Serve.

BACON AND BURGER BRUNCH

2 slices bacon, cut in half
¼ pound chopped meat
1 teaspoon lemon juice
Dash of salt
Leftover vegetables

Make patty out of chopped meat. Arrange bacon on meat. Sprinkle with lemon juice and salt. Broil until done, about 5–10 minutes. Mix with warmed leftover vegetables. Serve warm.

BURGANOODLE BASH

¼ pound chopped meat
Small amount elbow macaroni
⅛ teaspoon salt
1 small onion, chopped

Cook macaroni according to directions on package. Combine onion with chopped meat into patty and broil, with seasoning. Mix macaroni and meat. Serve.

TRIPE DELIGHT FANTASTIC

> 1 *small can tripe*
> *Margarine*
> *Salt*
> *Handful of kibble*

Preheat broiler. Brush tripe with margarine. Broil 10 minutes, turning frequently. Add seasoning. Serve warm, covered with kibble.

INSIDE CHICKEN, U.S.A.

> 1 *cup chicken innards*
> *Margarine or chicken fat*
> 1 *small onion*
> ⅛ *teaspoon salt*

Wash innards. Sauté, turning frequently, in margarine or chicken fat, with cut-up onion. Add seasoning. Cool and serve.

MEAT 'N' MUSHROOMS

> *Cut up leftover meat (beef, kidney, liver, lamb)*
> ½ *can mushroom soup, undiluted*
> *Grated cheese*
> *Handful of dog biscuits*

Add meat to warmed mushroom soup. Sprinkle with grated cheese and mix in dog biscuits. Serve warm.

BROILED LIVER

¼ *pound beef, calf, lamb, or chicken liver*
Margarine
Leftover vegetables

Preheat broiler, cut liver into pieces, brush with margarine, and broil about 4 minutes, turning once. Serve with warmed-up vegetables.

2

Hooray for Fillet!

Dogs love fish

Are you casting about for a good meat substitute for your dog? Well, put some bait on your hook and catch a juicy fish. That's right: dogs love fish. Now, a smart dog owner like you probably already knows this. Smart dogs know it and make good advantage of it, too. An ardent fisherman friend of mine once fished a whole day without getting a bite. He was about to pack up and go home when he observed his faithful dog take a sniff, inhale, then dive into the shallow water and emerge a few seconds later with a wriggling fish in his mouth. Like the faithful hound he was, he placed the fish at his grateful master's feet, and barked a few words of consolation. My fisherman friend was able to save face in front of his wife that eve-

. . . emerged with a wriggling fish in his mouth . . .

ning, and, needless to say, his super-smart dog was richly rewarded with a fresh fish dinner!

Fishy dishes make a good meal for dogs because they satisfy that old inherent canine drive for protein and iodine. Protein provides amino acids a dog needs for building and repairing of tissue and cells. Without these essential amino acids there would be no growth of new tissues and cells when needed, nor would there be as efficient repair of damaged tissue. The need for iodine is just as basic for our four-legged friends, since iodine is one of the essential minerals all dogs need in their system to aid in making glossy coats, combating anemia, and strengthening bones.

So fish is fine food for dogs, make no bones about it. I repeat: *Make no bones about it!* If you're going to cook fish for your dog, make sure that it's free of sharp bones. An easy way to do this is to grind the fish in your meat grinder or blender rather than stand and pick out bones one by one. Of course, you can avoid this do-it-yourself deboning process entirely by purchasing fish fillets, but unless your dog's share of the family budget is ample, the cost of bone-free fillets may be prohibitive. It's simple enough to grind the bones right into the fish via the meat-grinder method, which will not only make your dog less prone to a piercing bone, but will add an appreciable amount of health-giving calcium to his diet.

Losing your temper over your dog's distemper? There's no need to flounder around at your wit's end because a recent attack of distemper is causing your pet to view every meal with a fishy eye. Just cook a spot of fish for your dog. Now, fish is not a cure for distemper, but if your dog has any glandular disturbance after a bout with distemper (or *any* long illness), he can be helped along the path to good health with generous portions of fishy meals. And, as distasteful as it sounds to us humans, a combination of fish and meat in your dog's dinner will do wonders to help fortify his system against further serious ills.

The trick to remember is that, although fish is easily digested by dogs, it is not quite as nutritious as meat; therefore, if you are going to give your much-petted pet a dinner of fish, give him a heaping

Fish fill that old canine drive for protein and iodine

Canned fish has a strong odor

bowlful. Or give him more than one fish meal a week. Just make sure that when you substitute fish for meat there is more quantity in his portion. Some dog lovers feed fish to their pets twice a week all the time. This, of course, is up to your discretion and your dog's likes and dislikes.

Some tips on fish dishes, fellow dog lovers: Canned salmon, tuna, and mackerel are canine favorites, the reason being that these canned fishes have a strong odor, which is what dogs always nose around for.

You may serve fish cooked or cold, but if it is cooked, don't fry it. Bake it or broil it. And make sure that fish dishes are only lukewarm when you serve them, not hot. There's no sense burning your pet's tongue!

A final word: the main appeal of fish is as a flavor change. Dogs need changes in the flavor of their diet. Although they don't mind the same food meal after meal, you can have a healthier pet if you give him a change of flavor occasionally. Since flavor and smell are such an important part of their incentive to eat, a flavor change such as fish falls into the category of ensuring that your dog is well fed. Remember, it is better that he be well fed than fed up!

Next time your dog needs a change of dinner, tip your hat to the fisherman, and give a hearty "hooray" for fillet!

BROILED SALMON

¼ *pound canned salmon, drained*
½ *teaspoon fresh lemon juice, or its equivalent*
⅛ *teaspoon onion salt*
1 *teaspoon melted margarine*

Preheat broiler. Drain salmon. Place in shallow baking dish. Sprinkle with lemon juice, onion salt, and margarine. Broil until lightly browned. Serve warm.

FISH FIGHT

½ *can tuna*
2 *slices bacon*
1 *hard-cooked egg*
Milk

Cook bacon. Add tuna and diced egg, and enough milk to moisten. Top with pieces of bacon. Serve cold.

CHEESE AND MACKEREL

¼ *pound mackerel fillets*
2 *slices American cheese*
Margarine
Juice of ¼ fresh lemon

Preheat broiler. Cover fillets with cheese and broil in margarine. Squeeze juice of ¼ fresh lemon over fish and cheese. Broil about 4–5 minutes. Serve warm.

TOAST 'N' TUNA

1 *teaspoon margarine*
½ *teaspoon flour*
½ *small onion, diced*
½ *can tuna, drained*
¼ *cup milk*
2 *slices toast*

Heat oven to 400°. Melt margarine in saucepan. Stir in flour and onion. Add flour, if needed, to make solid consistency. Simmer 5 minutes, stirring occasionally. Add tuna. Place toast in baking dish. Add tuna mixture, cover with milk, and bake for 10 minutes. Serve warm.

SARDINE SUPREME

> 1 small can sardines
> Lettuce
> ½ tomato
> Vinegar
> Handful of kibble

Mash sardines with fork. Shred lettuce and cut tomato. Add lettuce and tomato to sardines. Pour about a capful of vinegar over mixture. Add kibble and serve.

CLAM-DIGGER SPECIAL*

> 1 small can clams
> Ketchup
> Lemon juice
> Kibble

Cut clams into small pieces. Mix with ketchup. Sprinkle lemon juice over mixture and add kibble. Serve.

SHRIMP SPECIAL, A LA ZOTTO*

> ¼ pound cooked fresh or canned shrimp
> 1 small can tomato purée
> Salt
> ¼ cup instant rice
> 4 crackers

Heat shrimp in tomato purée, adding salt. Mix with cooked instant rice. Crumble in crackers. Serve warm.

* Recipes marked with an asterisk (*) throughout are rewards and special treats (see Chapter 11).

BROILED WHITEFISH*

1 small whitefish
Margarine
Milk
Flour
Leftover vegetables

Preheat broiler. Split whitefish and remove bones. Brush with margarine. Broil until slightly brown. Heat milk and add enough flour to make smooth sauce. Add sauce to fish and serve with warmed-up vegetables. Serve warm.

FISH PUDDING*

Leftover cooked fish
Margarine
½ cup warm milk
½ cup bread crumbs
Salt
1 egg

Mash fish. Melt margarine in milk and add bread crumbs and salt. Add fish. Beat egg well and add. Bake at 350° F. until done, about 5 minutes.

TUNOODLE

½ can tuna, drained
Small amount of wide noodles or elbow macaroni
¼ green pepper, diced
½ small onion, diced
Handful of dog biscuits
½ cup milk

Cook noodles according to directions on package. Add to tuna, pepper, and onion. Add milk and mix. Cover with handful of dog biscuits and serve cold.

3
Soup's On!

The older a dog gets, the choosier he gets

It is a bone of contention among many dog owners, not to mention dogs themselves, whether or not soup makes a good main course for the heel-and-sit set. Well, my pets, let your K-9 be your guide! If he greedily slurps down soup, fine. If he doesn't, it needs more cooking. The point is that soup is a terrific meal for dogs.

Why? Well, in addition to its appeal as a flavor favorite, it has a strong psychological appeal. A psychologist friend of mine (of the Pavlovian school, naturally) once told me that she makes a succulent stew for her Irish wolfhound on the average of once a week. Perhaps because he was Irish he wolfed down the stew, but she likes to think that it was a psychological bluff. How? Well, McGillicuddy (the dog, not the psychologist) detested spinach. Now, I ask you, what son of Erin in his right mind doesn't detest spinach in favor of meat and potatoes? So, our Freudian friend would disguise a portion of spinach in a palatable stew, and faster than McGillicuddy could bark, "Begorra!" he would demolish his bowl of steaming stew.

If your dog doesn't like a particular food, no matter how good it is for him, he isn't going to lick his chops over it even if it is prepared by Oscar of the Waldorf. There are plenty of foods to choose from rather than those he doesn't like. Of course, if it is necessary for your dog to have a special food or diet, and he just despises it, you may build up his acceptance of it by giving him small samples of the food cleverly camouflaged in a delectable soup. Although soup may be a good psychological bluff, don't make the mistake of forcing it down his throat when he refuses it, or you may find him retaliating and making a fine feast of your favorite shoes!

If you have an old dog, try soup. Soup is a great psychological bluff for him too. A well-cooked soup softens necessary meats to allow for easier digestion. Also, the older a dog gets, the choosier he gets. Soup, naturally, allows meaty flavor to seep through to other required, and often rejected, food for older dogs. Thus he is sidetracked into thinking that he's getting an all-meat dinner without those nasty vegetables he's grown to know and hate.

But the most important thing to remember about soup is the value in its aroma. The fragrant smell of a well-made soup acts on the digestive juices of the dog's stomach and starts them flowing. This prepares the stomach for the work it must do. The important thing to remember is that your dog's stomach juices must be flowing properly so that he can digest his dinner easily. The aroma of food cooking, especially a well-flavored, stewy soup, completes this process of instigating the digestive flow. So don't forget: The way to a dog's stomach is through his nose!

Some tips on soup making: Soups for dogs should be thick and stewy rather than thin and watery. This enables him to chew his way through a meal, giving his jaws the workout they need. When you add meat to soup, make sure that it is lightly browned (sautéed) first. This enables the meat's flavor to permeate the broth better.

*The fragrant aroma of soup prepares the stomach
for the work it must do . . .*

Also, you may want to soak the meat in a lightly covered jar of cold water for 8 hours, *then* sauté it. The flavor of the meat will be in the water, which should be included in the broth. In winter use more fatty meats than lean meats in soup making, since fat produces much-needed heat in the dog's body. And remember that dogs, just like their feline enemies, love fish. So make chowders for your dog. Be sure, though, in making a fishy soup, that all fish is boned thoroughly.

A word to the wise, friends: Soup's on! If you want to make sure that your dog *stays* in the doghouse, give him potfuls of soup, and don't spare the horse meat!

"Beau-ootiful soo-oop! Beau-ootiful soo-oop . . . !
Adapted from the classic Wedgwood design,

TOMATO AND BEAN SOUP

   2 strips bacon
   1 small can pork and beans
   1 small can tomato soup, undiluted
   Handful of kibble

Fry bacon and crumble. Mix pork and beans with tomato soup.
Heat. Add bacon to soup mixture. Add kibble. Serve warm.

EASY MEAT-BALL STEW

   ½ can cream of chicken soup
   ½ cup water
   ½ pound chopped meat
   ¼ cup leftover vegetables

Blend soup and water. Make meat balls and add to soup. Cook over
low flame until soup boils. Stir in vegetables. Simmer. Serve cool.

BOUILLON VEGETABLE SOUP

   1 beef bouillon cube
   1¼ cups water
   ½ cup vegetables
   2½ cups dog biscuits
   ½ cup milk

Soo-oop of the e-e-evening . . . Beautiful, beautiful soup!"
Flaxman's "Dance of the Hours"

Dissolve bouillon cube in boiling water. Add vegetables that are leftovers from your own dinner. Stir in biscuits. When mixture has cooled, add milk and stir.

CHUNKY MEAT SOUP

1½ cup leftover lean beef, chicken, or lamb cut in chunks
Enough water to keep ingredients moist
1 cup dry dog biscuits
Dash of onion or garlic salt
Grated cheese

Add chunks of meat into simmering water. Cook 2 minutes. Remove from heat, cool, and stir in biscuits and seasoning. Sprinkle with grated cheese. Serve.

MEAT-BALL SOUP

1 can meat balls in gravy for dogs
1 teaspoon chopped green pepper
2 tablespoons grated or chopped carrot
Margarine
¼ cup milk or water

Sauté pepper and carrot in a small amount of margarine until tender. Gradually add milk and can of dog meat balls. Heat until warm. Serve warm.

The way to a dog's stomach is through his nose . . .

FISH CHOWDER

> ½ *pound boned haddock*
> ¾ *cup peeled, sliced potatoes*
> 1 *small onion, chopped*
> ½ *cup water*
> ½ *tablespoon butter*
> *Salt*
> *Milk*

Cut fish into small pieces. Place in saucepan with potatoes, onion, water and cook for 15 minutes, well covered. Stir in butter and seasoning. Add enough milk to make a broth. Serve.

BACON SOUP

> 2 *or 3 strips bacon*
> ½ *can dog food*
> ½ *cup milk*
> *Dash of salt*

Cook bacon in saucepan until crisp, then break into pieces. Pour off fat. Add dog food and break up into small pieces with fork. Gradually add milk and salt. Heat thoroughly and serve.

CLAM CHOWDER*

   1 *small can clams*
   2 *strips bacon*
   1 *small onion, chopped*
   1 *cup peeled, sliced potatoes*
   Dash of salt
   ½ *cup water*
   1 *cup milk*
   Handful of dog biscuits

Cook bacon, onion, potatoes, and salt in water, about 15 minutes, or until potatoes are tender. Add clams, milk, and dog biscuits. Stir. Cool and serve in bowl.

Allow soup to cool . . .

THICK LAMB SOUP

½ *pound cubed lamb*
¼ *teaspoon salt*
½ *cup chopped onions*
½ *stalk celery, sliced*
⅓ *cup instant rice*

Simmer lamb cubes, salt, onions, and celery in water, about 10 minutes or until well done. While meat is cooking, prepare instant rice. Add rice to meat. Cool to lukewarm and serve.

VICTORY STEW

¼ *cup broad noodles*
½ *cup vegetable soup*
½ *cup water*
Handful of kibble

Prepare noodles as directed on package. Heat soup and water, but do not boil. Add noodles. When cool enough to serve add handful of kibble. Serve.

4

A Little Starch Around the Collar, Please!

They must eat what we give them . . .

Is there anyone in the balcony who believes that starch shouldn't be included in a dog's dinner? ("Oh, but it sounds so terribly *fattening!*" a lorgnette-carrying Long Island matron once exclaimed when confronted with this question.) Well, your dog's dinner would be terribly bland if you didn't include a little starch. No one is saying that there should be a lot of starch in every meal, but there is some definite value in including starch in his dinner. ·

Starch adds variety. Variety in form. Variety in flavor. Variety in eye appeal. Dogs love a variety of density and texture in their meals, as do humans. Our four-legged friends get a big charge out of varied textures in the same mouthful of food. Also, being the sensory-oriented animals they are, they are pursuaded by flavor and smell. And, the starchy fillers add flavor to meals. Eye appeal is just as important, too. Since dogs can't make their own selection of food, they must eat what we give them. So why not make dinner a little eye-appealing. An eye-appealing meal is a pleasant meal!

But the most important value of fillers, or starches, is that of catalyst in the digestive process. In short, the fillers serve as an excellent laxative. Meat, fish, eggs, and cheese are proteins, and they are highly desirable in the diet, but, like any food, they leave wastes that are not discharged in the normal process of elimination. If these wastes remain too long, they may be harmful. The fillers act as a destructive agent for them, helping to speed their elimination. On the other hand, protein acts as a counterbalance for the wastes left by starchy foods. Therefore, protein and starch have value in complementing each other.

Naturally, you shouldn't overdo the use of fillers. Too much starch is not good for your dog. The proportion of starch and protein should be balanced. The factors involved in determining how much filler to be fed to your dog are mainly dependent upon the size and activity of the animal. The more active he is, the more starch he can digest.

What does it mean if your dog turns up his nose at the roughage you serve him? Well, it can mean a couple of things. First, vegetables, either cooked or raw, are not his natural food. Dogs are carnivores. Thus, their natural instinct is to eat meat rather than vegetables. Second, you may be feeding him too much roughage; thus he rejects the vegetables you place before him. Use a little caution and common sense, and don't feed him too much filler.

The best starchy vegetables you can feed your dog are carrots, beets, onions, and rice. And by the way, many dog owners feel that onions are a natural wonder drug for dogs. Onions seem to be an extremely good remedy for a dog's head colds, since they help him to keep his air passages open and his nasal membranes moist.

Macaroni and spaghetti have their place in your dog's dinner fare, but the general rule in serving *pasta* is "not too much and not too often."

An eye-appealing meal is a pleasant meal

A few quick hints in preparing starchy fillers for your dog: Unless you mix the starchy foods and vegetables with his meat, and mix them well, he won't eat them. You may want to camouflage these vegetables in a tasty soup (see Chapter 3, "Soup's On!") or by pouring gravy or chicken, lamb, or bacon fat over the entire dinner in order to add a zesty flavor. Also, don't hesitate to throw in a handful of dog biscuits or kibble to add texture. Rice and macaroni have a tendency to be a little constipating for your dog (so does meat), but the root vegetables, like carrots, when added to the basic meal

A little starch won't do him any harm . . .

act as a perfect laxative. And, when you do serve carrots, grind or mash them first before serving.

Your choice of roughage for your dog can make quite a difference in his health. Don't forget to include these fillers as well as protein and vitamins. If your dog does finish his dinner with a little telltale bit of starch around his collar don't be upset. Chances are it won't harm him one bit!

MACARONI SALAD

> 6 ounces cooked macaroni
> 2 hard-cooked eggs
> Creamed cottage cheese

Slice eggs. Mix with macaroni and some cottage cheese. Serve cold.

PINEAPPLE SUPREME

> ¼ cup crushed pineapple, drained
> 2 slices bacon
> Cream cheese
> Handful of kibble

Cook bacon until crisp, break into bits, and add to pineapple and cream cheese mixture. Sprinkle with kibble and serve.

TOMATO TREAT

Handful of bread crumbs
1 teaspoon melted margarine
Dash of salt
Dash of minced onion
1 tomato, drained
Handful of kibble
Water

Combine all ingredients except kibble and water, heat. Add kibble and moisten with water. Serve.

SPECIAL BACON AND EGGS

2 hard-cooked eggs
2 slices bacon
Creamed cottage cheese

Fry bacon and crumble. Chop eggs and add to crisp bacon bits. Add cottage cheese to mixture and serve.

The more active he is, the more starch he can digest . . .

SPINACH SALAD*

> 2 strips bacon
> ½ small onion
> ½ small can spinach, drained
> 1 hard-cooked egg
> 2 slices toast

Cook bacon and remove from skillet. Cook onion in bacon fat for 2 minutes. Mix onion and bacon bits with warmed spinach. Cut up egg and add to mixture. Break up toast and mix in. Serve warm.

CARROT AND ONION GLAZE*

> 1 small can whole carrots, drained
> 1 small onion, sliced
> ¼ cup syrup
> ¼ cup apple juice
> Handful of dog biscuits

Heat carrots and onion. Pour off liquid. Heat syrup and juice. Stir until thick syrup forms. Add carrots and onion to syrup and stir gently until glazed. Add dog biscuits and serve warm.

Pour gravy or chicken, lamb, or bacon fat over the entire dinner . . .

DOGWICHES

¼ pound chopped meat
1 canned tomato, drained
Dry onion-soup mix
Kibble
1 slice toast

Sauté meat. Mix with tomato, onion-soup mix, and kibble. Serve over toast.

HOLLYWOOD COTTAGE CHEESE

Prepared wheat biscuits
Creamed cottage cheese
Cucumber slices

Break up 1 or 2 squares of prepared wheat biscuits and combine with some creamed cottage cheese. Mix in some cucumber slices and serve cold.

BEET TREAT

½ small can diced beets, drained
¼ cup cooked instant rice
Leftover beef, lamb, chicken
Handful of kibble
Milk

Warm beets. Mix with rice and meat. Add kibble. Moisten with milk and serve warm.

COTTAGE CHEESE CARESS

¼ cup cottage cheese
¼ cup grated carrot
Chopped lettuce
Leftover beef, lamb, chicken
Beef, lamb, or chicken fat

Mix cheese, carrot, lettuce, meat. Heat fat and pour over mixture. Serve.

5
Canine Casanova

Prepare yourself for a whirlwind social season

If you're the lucky dog owner who has a handsome and extremely adult male dog, then prepare yourself for a whirlwind social season! Any *femme fatale* who casts her eye on your male dog won't resist making a pitch to be the first bitch on his list!

Now, my dear dog owners, the important thing to remember at this exciting time is that when your dog starts roving you'd better stock in a full larder of nourishing food. Yes, when your male dog gets that gleam in his eye, and he begins to tango into the kitchen for breakfast each morning, you better start feeding him all the nourishing food he'll eat. After all, it's tiring being Rudolph Valentino!

First of all, the amorous male needs lots of meat. He's doing a man's work, and he needs a man's food. Plenty of meat will keep him both strong and lean. Make sure, too, that he gets plenty of exercise so that his flesh remains firm and hard. When he's parked in the moonlight with a cute date, he'd better not be too fat and soft. If she's a particular bitch (and what female dog isn't?), she's liable to turn her cheek to his anxious sniffings.

Obviously this would be a blow to his male ego. And your dog certainly should not have any deflation of ego at this time! He should be in the right frame of mind for procreating. Perhaps he didn't tell you, when you last sat in front of the fireplace together, that this business of dating is pretty rough on him psychologically. He's probably run into several kinds of girls—those who just tease him with a little persuasive paw-holding, those who indulge in fancy doings with just any dog because that's the way to remain popular, and the "girl-next-door" dog, who is selective about her boy friends. Thus this whole dating system can be quite confusing and frustrating for him.

If you find him mooning around, unable to eat properly because he's frustrated—some bitch is teasing him beyond the point of endurance, or he's the victim of unrequited love—you should do something about it. Above all, make sure that he eats properly and regularly. Don't force him to eat, but if he's in the middle of a heavy date life, feed him two nourishing meals a day. Give him plenty of meat, milk, eggs, cottage cheese, liver, and oily fish. These foods are full of Vitamin E, which, I'm told, is sex food.

But maybe your dog still has a little of the wolf in him and is straining at the leash to get *intime* with his girl friend. Well, before he starts putting on his white tie and tail, make sure that he rests for at least an hour after dinner. Even if he has a big date with the best-looking bitch in town, make your dog rest a little.

And if you have a pedigreed stud dog, now you can rent him for fun and profit.

Yes, the stud fees are high these days, and you certainly can make a profit on his fun. Why, I know one owner of a prolific dog who was able to send his son to veterinary school on the profit he made in stud fees!

Make sure that he gets plenty of exercise

Now is the time when you'll be exhibiting your stud dog at shows, so make sure that he puts his best paw forward. He should be at top strength and virility so that he'll get plenty of fancy "come hither" looks. Feed him well, and scrub him, too. He doesn't have to look like Cary Grant to be appealing, but if he's well groomed and in good physical condition, any bitch will find him attractive. Remember, it's much easier to groom him well if he's been eating well.

Now that your dog is prowling around the neighborhood, the most important thing is his health, and feeding him properly helps him maintain his health. Remember this, and there's no doubt that your dog will be the Casanova of the crowd for a long time to come!

SALMON STEW*

> 2 tablespoons margarine
> 1½ tablespoons flour
> ½ teaspoon salt
> 1 cup milk
> 8 ounces salmon, drained
> Leftover vegetables
> Dog biscuits

Melt margarine in double boiler. Add flour and salt. Add milk slowly. Stir constantly to prevent lumps. Cook until smooth. Add salmon and leftover vegetables, cooking until fish is warm. Serve sprinkled with dog biscuits.

This business of dating is pretty rough on him psychologically

Feed him two nourishing meals a day

HIGH-PROTEIN DINNER

1 can dog food
Cottage cheese
Sour cream
1 hard-cooked egg, sliced
Warm water

Mash dog food in bowl. Add some cottage cheese and sour cream and sliced egg. Pour some warm water over mixture and combine. Serve.

Rent him for fun and profit

LIVER AND TOMATO DINNER

>*4 ounces liver*
>*1 cup tomatoes, drained*
>*Leftover vegetables*
>*½ cup milk*

Broil liver until slightly browned. Cut into pieces. Mix with tomatoes and warmed leftover vegetables. Pour milk over mixture. Serve.

QUICK-ENERGY DINNER

>*2 eggs*
>*Handful of dog biscuits*

Soft-boil eggs (4 minutes). Place in bowl and add dog biscuits. Mix and serve.

DOG DIP*

>*1 package dry onion-soup mix*
>*½ small package cream cheese*
>*Handful of dog biscuits*

Combine dry onion soup and cream cheese (softened at room temperature). Add biscuits. Serve cold.

LIVER AND EGGS

4 ounces chicken liver
Margarine
2 hard-cooked eggs
Cream cheese

Sauté liver in margarine. Combine with eggs and mix in blender or with fine blade of food chopper until well mixed. Blend in cream cheese. Serve cold.

DRIED BEEF

1 tablespoon margarine
1 tablespoon flour
½ cup milk
¼ pound dried beef
½ small can asparagus

Stir flour in melted margarine. Add milk. Cook until smooth, stirring constantly. Fold in dried beef. Mix in asparagus. Serve warm.

CANINE OMELET

Leftover meat
¼ green pepper
2 eggs
Margarine

Dice meat and green pepper, add to eggs as they are being scrambled in margarine. Serve warm.

CHICKEN SURPRISE

3 ounces cooked chicken
1 hard-cooked egg
½ small onion, sliced
¼ cup diced celery
Creamed cottage cheese

Slice chicken and egg. Combine with onion and celery. Add cottage cheese and mix well. Serve cold.

ENTRAIL DELIGHT

Assorted beef or chicken innards
Chicken fat or bacon fat
Cottage cheese
Leftover vegetables

Place innards in saucepan and cover with water. Cook for 5 minutes, or until warm (do not boil). Put meat in bowl, add cottage cheese and warmed leftover vegetables. Mix and serve.

6

Pregnant Paws

So you're going to have a litter!

So you're going to have a litter! Well, congratulations. But before you start knitting litter things, or buying cigars for your canine friends, sit down and plan the expectant mother's meals with a little care and common sense.

There's no need for her to maintain her girlish figure . . .

Let's be scientific about it. The important thing to remember is that the mother must now eat enough food, not only to provide ample nourishment for the unborn pups, but to maintain her own health. Mamma must be strong enough to manufacture new tissue for her forthcoming issue.

And remember, there's no need for her to maintain her girlish figure any more. On the other hand, Mamma should not be allowed to get foolishly fat. She should be on the "fat" side rather than lean and languid, though. Keep her pregnantly plump rather than schoolgirl skinny.

But don't rush into the kitchen as soon as you hear that she's in the family way. There's no need to change her normal meal consumption for the first four or five weeks of her pregnancy. During the sixth week her food consumption should be gradually increased. If Mom is used to eating one meal a day, feed her two. If she usually eats two meals, just make them larger.

Her meals should contain plenty of Vitamins A and D. The foods that are high in Vitamin A are: butter, cream, whole milk, dog biscuit, egg yolk and white, spinach, and meat. Cheese, tomatoes, carrots, kidney, liver, thin-leafed green vegetables, raw cabbage, pineapple, and peaches have a significant amount of Vitamin A too.

Vitamin D can be found in butter, whole milk, egg yolk, liver, sardines, and cod-liver oil.

Now don't turn up your nose, but pregnant dogs must have cod-liver oil. That old fishy spring tonic *you've* hated ever since you were knee high to the oven door is a must for your dog. Cod-liver oil helps prevent rickets in the pups. Try giving Mom one to three tablespoonfuls, depending on her size, every day all through her pregnancy and during the nursing period. And if you begin to look like a home-grown Lucretia Borgia as you approach her with the spoonful of cod-liver oil, try your own mother's trick of camouflage. Put the oil in her dinner and chances are she won't even notice the difference.

Another worth-while source of minerals for the pregnant dog is fish. Boiled whitefish with a thickened flour and milk sauce is a good brood food (see Chapter 2, "Hooray for Fillet!").

When she's about to deliver, you may want to remember these few hints. Mamma may reject her last meal before the long walk to the launching pad. This is not uncommon and should give no cause for worry. After all, with the load that's on her mind, who's got time to think of food? She may, though, want a dash of cold milk during the whelping. Give it to her. It helps make the delivery easier.

If her labor has been prolonged, add a spot of brandy to the milk. Also, make sure that there's plenty of cold fresh water at paw for a chaser!

The long walk to the launching pad . . .

Add a spot of brandy to the milk . . .

Between arrivals, or after delivery, Mom is bound to be a little tuckered out. She'll lick your hand profusely if you give her a little warm (not hot) food. Or reward her with a piece of candy or a lump of sugar, providing she's the sugar-daddy type. The sugar will give her the instant energy and strength she needs after the ordeal she's been bearing.

Well, now that the family has arrived safely, and Mamma has started her job of taking care of them, you can run out and buy those cigars, but don't take too long, the fun is just beginning!

SALAD DAYS

> 1 *peach*
> Cottage cheese
> Salad greens

Cut peach into small pieces. Mix with cottage cheese. Add to salad greens. Serve.

LAMB 'N' BACON

Leftover lamb
3 strips bacon
Minced onion
Dog biscuits

Cut bacon in half and cook. When bacon is nearly done, add pieces of lamb mixed with onion. Cook about 2 minutes. Serve with broken-up dog biscuits.

GRAHAM CRACKERS 'N' MILK

Break up graham crackers in bowl. Moisten with milk. Top with your dog's favorite fresh fruit. Serve.

HUNKS AND CHUNKS

Leftover meats (combination of beef, lamb, chicken, etc.)
1 small onion, sliced
Leftover vegetables
1 can chicken with rice soup, undiluted
Handful of kibble

Mix all ingredients. Heat until warm. Add kibble. Serve.

Mom is bound to be a little tuckered out . . .

TOMATO TEMPTER

1 fresh tomato
Leftover beef, lamb, chicken
Handful of kibble
Lettuce

Cut an x on top of tomato nearly through and pull tomato open to form a cup. Add mixture of meat and kibble. Top with shredded lettuce. Serve.

EGG ZACTLY

2 eggs
Minced onion
2 slices toast

Boil eggs 4 minutes, place in bowl, and sprinkle on minced onion. Break up toast and mix with eggs. Serve warm.

KING CHICKEN*

2 slices buttered toast
Some slices leftover chicken
Tomato slices
Grated cheese

Place buttered toast in broiler. Place chicken and tomato on toast. Sprinkle liberally with cheese. Broil until cheese is brown. Serve warm.

VARIETY SALAD

Leftover meats (combination of beef, lamb, chicken, etc.)
½ small green pepper, chopped
½ small onion, chopped
¼ can mixed Chinese vegetables, drained
Kibble
Bacon fat

Toss and mix ingredients. Pour warm bacon fat over mixture. Serve.

NICE RICE

1 bouillon cube
¼ cup cooked instant rice
1 small onion, chopped
Leftover vegetables

Melt bouillon cube in small amount of warm water. Add rice and onion. Add leftover vegetables and mix all ingredients well. Serve warm.

CHEESE FRIEZE

Margarine
Grated cheese
½ package dry onion-soup mix
½ cup flour
Milk

Mix all ingredients except milk. Pour into pan and bake at 375° for 10 minutes, or until done. Moisten with milk and serve warm.

7
Good to the Last Drop!

Calories don't count

Want to help ensure that the new mother's milk is good to the last drop? Well, there are a few simple things to remember when cooking for the lactating dog. The general rule of thumb is to cook plain and hearty meals that can be easily digested. Don't worry too much about the calorie count. Mamma should be fed all she wants. It is better that she be a little plump right now. After all, lactation drains a lot out of her!

The secret to successful lactation is keeping the new mother strong. Therefore, any food that strengthens her for the chore of providing chow for her crew is to her advantage.

Mamma must provide large quantities of milk

Naturally, there are some foods that are more advantageous than others. High on the list of milk-producing mainstays are meat, eggs, liver, cocoa, bread and butter, simple vegetables, and, of course, milk itself.

Some authorities contend that for the first few days after the stork's visit Mamma should be fed moderately. The reason for this is that no large amounts of milk are required by the new pups during this early stage. After this the quantity of food for Mom should be increased so that she can produce large quantities of milk. After all, you wouldn't want dear old Mom to be an udder failure!

Immediately after whelping, Mamma may be fed three medium-sized meals (smaller quantities than the usual serving) of fairly light food. Bread and milk, milk and egg custard, or meals with a milky base fall into this category. You may want to serve her boiled eggs on the second day after birth. Full-course meals can be served after the second day, if there are no complications in her milk giving. One good source says that a mother with a litter of hungry pups bothering her constantly should have four meals a day, with the last meal being as close to bedtime as possible. If she has no complications in feeding her young, simple, full meals should provide enough milk for her mob. The process of nursing stimulates the flow of milk, and the full meals do the rest.

If Mamma doesn't have enough milk for her family, lactation can be encouraged by feeding her a broth made of milk food, like malted-milk powder mixed with water or milk. Or she may have a yen for dog biscuits soaked in milk. Remember to keep a fresh supply of water for her at all times. The more liquid she drinks, the more liquid she can dispense to her ravenous brood.

And when it's time for the milk supply to be stopped, here's what you can do. If the pups have been weaned in the normal length of time (about six weeks), Mom will have naturally exhausted her milk supply. Six weeks of milk giving will make even the hardiest of mothers weak and drained dry!

Sometimes the milk flow must be ebbed sooner than it runs its course. If the litter dies, or the mother is found to be unfit to nurse her own brood, there is no need for her to lactate. Then the flow of milk may be halted by taking some simple steps.

First, Mamma should be fed small amounts of food, with only limited liquids at each meal. This, obviously, is the opposite of the meal pattern to be followed for dogs who must be at full strength in order to lactate. Second, a dose of Epsom salts, or some other salt solution, which your friendly veterinarian may prescribe, will help

Lactation takes its toll . . .

Take good care of Mamma dog during these delicate days . . .

halt Mom's milk supply. The consensus of opinion indicates that this is the simplest way to delactate your dog if everything is normal.

Some general information to keep in mind when preparing food for the lactating dog: It has been discovered by many authorities that liver produces more milk than even lean beef. This does not mean that you should eliminate lean beef from her meals entirely! On the contrary, beef *should be included* for its many other food values. And when you do cook beef for Mamma, wait until a few days *after* she begins giving milk. Her system won't be able to take beef until then.

An important factor in making for a good milk supply is including a significant amount of fat in Mamma's meals. Milky foods or bits of bread and butter in your dog's dinner can aid in increasing her supply of fats.

Some sources indicate that the new mother should be fed a small amount of milk of magnesia the day after she gives birth. Why? Well, as you know, a mamma dog eats her afterbirth. This laxative dose helps her to discharge the placenta in the normal course of elimination.

Another important point of information is to remember that the full complement of vitamins should be included in Mamma's diet. Especially Vitamin B. It has been proved by veterinarians that lactating dogs need much more Vitamin B than they do normally.

Foods like yeast, wheat germ, and muscle meat should be included in great quantities to provide this vitamin need.

And a parting thought: Take good care of Mamma during these delicate days. Patience is a virtue, and sometimes a luxury, but with the lactating dog it is a necessity. With this thought in mind you should have little trouble making her dinner.

MEAT DELIGHT

¼ pound chopped meat
½ can (5 ounces) condensed tomato soup
¼ cup milk

Make patty out of meat. Broil until brown. Heat soup, stirring often. Add meat to soup. Blend in warm milk. Serve warm.

COUNTRY DINNER

½ small can whole-kernel corn
1 chicken or beef bouillon cube
Dash of salt
1 cup milk
½ small onion, sliced
½ tablespoon flour
Handful of kibble

Cook corn, bouillon, salt, milk, and onion 10 minutes. (Add water if necessary to keep from sticking to saucepan.) Add flour. Cook 5 minutes. Add kibble and serve warm.

SPECIAL VEGETABLE DINNER*

1 small can peas
Grated cheese
½ can condensed cream of mushroom soup
1 small can evaporated milk

Heat peas. Sprinkle with cheese. Pour mixture of soup and evaporated milk over top of peas. Bake in 350° F. oven for 25 minutes. Serve warm.

QUICK CANINE CUSTARD

½ cup milk
1 tablespoon custard powder

Place measuring cup of milk into a pan of hot (not boiling) water for 2 minutes. Add custard powder. Stir until dissolved. Pour into bowl. Serve after standing for 10 minutes.

AFTER-WHELPING DINNER

2 slices white bread and butter
½ cup warm milk
½ cup evaporated milk

Break bread into small pieces. Add to warm milk and evaporated milk mixture. Serve warm.

EGG CUSTARD*

⅓ cup evaporated milk
1 cup hot water
2 eggs, slightly beaten
Dash of salt
½ teaspoon vanilla extract

Combine milk and water. Stir into eggs. Stir in salt and vanilla. Pour into greased bowl. Place in pan filled with hot water. Bake in 325° F. oven for 1 hour or until knife inserted at center comes out clean. Serve chilled.

MILK-MAKER MEAL

½ pound chopped meat
1 small can onions, drained
Handful of dog biscuits
1 can vegetable soup, undiluted
Milk

Sauté meat. Mix in onions, biscuits, vegetable soup. Add some milk. Serve warm.

LIVER SPECIAL

Liver
1 small onion, sliced
Leftover vegetables
Sour cream
Dog biscuits

Broil pieces of liver until slightly browned. Add sliced onion and warmed leftover vegetables. Cover with sour cream and dog biscuits. Serve.

BLITZED MEAT

½ small can evaporated milk
1 egg
Dash of salt
1 tablespoon margarine
½ cup chopped meat

Place milk and egg in bowl, beat until smooth. Add salt. Melt margarine. Pour in egg mixture. Add meat and cook until set. Serve warm.

QUICK DINNER

1 can dog food
Milk
Leftover vegetables
Bacon fat

Add milk to dog food and mix thoroughly. Warm leftover vegetables and mix in. Pour warm bacon fat over mixture. Serve warm.

8

For a Fitter Litter!

The simplest way to feed a puppy is to let his mother do it for you . . .

There's no need to get all a-twitter about making sure that you have a fitter litter than you've ever had before. Puppy feeding is not as difficult as it seems to be.

The simplest way to feed a puppy is to let his mother do it for you! Natural milk from the dam is the best food a pup can have. Eventually, though, you must tend to the feeding yourself. In a normal situation, once the pup has been weaned, the job of preparing meals is solely up to you. Before weaning you have a part-time meal preparation job, and sometimes a full-time job.

If the mother dies, or the quantity and quality of her milk are inadequate to feed her litter, then you must get a foster mother who is lactating properly to provide bed and board for the new brood. If there are no foster mothers available, then *you* are faced with the problem of being a canine nursemaid.

By this time the puppies are ready to be weaned

This is a trying situation, but it is not one that is really difficult. The object in playing mother to a litter of pups is to keep their bellies full for as long as possible, without actually forcing them to eat.

If you must undertake to prepare all the meals for the newborn pups right from their birth, the first three weeks are quite trying. This is when they need the most attention.

During the first two weeks pups must be fed every two hours, around the clock. The usual regimen is a straight diet of slightly warmed milk food (malted-milk powder and milk or water). Beginning with the third week, feeding takes place every three hours and continues on this schedule for one month, then every four hours for two more weeks. By this time the pups are ready to be weaned.

If the pups are being fed *au naturel* from Mamma, it is during the third week, or when their teeth begin to appear, that some dog owners begin augmenting her milk with solid food. This can be scraped raw beef served at body temperature rather than refrigerator-cold. The usual serving on the first day of this switch to solid food is two teaspoonfuls served several hours apart in addition to the usual milk ration. The second day the pups may have a little more of this scraped beef, perhaps three or four spoonfuls. Increasing amounts of raw meat may be fed quite rapidly. By the middle of the fourth week the meat can be finely ground so that the chewing process may be initiated.

At this time cereals (cooked oatmeal, prepared wheat biscuit) and dried bread or toast soaked in milk may be served with the meat. The pups may be fed small portions of this solid food three or four times a day in addition to their milk diet, even before they are weaned. By the time they are ready to be weaned (about the sixth week after birth) they may be ready for a dog biscuit soaked in milk along with the meat meal.

By this time the pups are ready to eat a great many other foods that lend variety and nourishment to their rapidly growing bodies. Cottage cheese, soft-boiled eggs, lamb broth, spinach, and tomatoes are some of the foods on which pups will thrive.

From the time the pup is weaned until he is three months old, he is fed a minimum of four times a day. When he reaches three months until he is six months, the number of meals is reduced to a minimum of three a day. And from six months to a year he gets

Four meals a day

"It's too salty."

fed twice a day. After he is one year old, one or two meals a day are sufficient.

Some general information that may help! If your pups are orphans and you must feed them on cow's milk, add cream to it. The consistency of the cow's milk is not as rich as the dog's. The pup requires a great deal of cream, since 70 per cent of his energy is derived from fat at this stage in his life. Food that is somewhat constipating should be fed to the pup, so that you won't have too much trouble cleaning up after him if he is still not housebroken. This is true of any house dog. If you feed your dog salty or dry foods, he'll be tempted to drink a great deal, and perhaps he will stain a carpet or floor with his feces.

One way to help the puppy start eating from a shallow pan is to have him lick your fingers first, then put your finger right into the food so that he continues to lick your finger and the food, too. Another way is to spread a thin layer of butter or margarine on the bottom of the pan, then, as he starts licking it, pour the food or milk right into it.

There are many things you will learn through experience with your own pups, but for a fitter litter remember: patience and common sense will get you through the early stages. Get out that baby bottle, and happy nursing!

NOTE: These recipes are for the weaned pup. They are arranged so that the first few are for the pup that has been only recently weaned, while the remainder are for older pups.

NEAT MEAT

Lean beef
1 slice bread and butter
Milk

Grind meat thoroughly. Break bread and butter into small pieces and mix with meat. Moisten with milk. Serve.

EGG TREAT

2 eggs
1 slice bread and butter
Milk

Cook eggs 20 minutes. Chop and combine with broken-up bread and butter. Add milk and serve.

FORMULA NO. 8

¼ cup milk
¼ cup evaporated milk
1 egg yolk

Mix milk and evaporated milk. Beat egg yolk and add to milk. Serve cold.

FISH DISH

Salmon, drained
¼ cup light cream
Lettuce, chopped

Mash up small amount of drained salmon in bowl. Mix with cream. Add some chopped lettuce. Serve.

TEETHING DINNER

> 1 slice whole-wheat bread
> Raw lean beef
> Milk

Toast whole-wheat bread and break into small pieces. Mix with meat. Place toast and meat mixture in bowl of milk. Serve.

DAIRY FEAST

> Prepared wheat biscuit
> Cottage cheese
> ½ cup milk

Crumble some prepared wheat biscuit into small pieces. Mix with a little cottage cheese. Add milk and serve.

POPEYED PUPPY

> 2 ounces chopped meat
> Margarine
> ½ cup warmed spinach
> ½ cup tomatoes, drained
> Light cream

Sauté meat in margarine. Combine with spinach and tomatoes. Add cream and serve.

TOAST OF THE TOWN

> 1 slice whole-wheat toast
> 2 ounces cooked oatmeal
> Light cream

Crumble toast into small pieces. Add to oatmeal. Place in bowl and pour light cream over mixture. Serve warm.

HOME-STYLE BOUILLON DINNER

1 bouillon cube
½ cup warm water
Leftover vegetables, warmed
Shredded raw meat

Melt bouillon in water. Add to mixture of vegetables and meat. Serve warm.

FULL-COURSE DINNER

¼ pound ground meat
½ small onion, chopped
Margarine
¼ cup milk
¼ cup evaporated milk
Handful of soda crackers

Sauté meat and onions in margarine. Place in bowl. Add milk and evaporated milk mixture. Crumble soda crackers over mixture. Serve warm.

9

Put on the Dog

Floor it!

One hundred years ago it was quite common to see the giant Conestoga wagons crossing the Great Plains headed for California. Quite often the head of the family would walk in front of the wagon leading the horses. And, invariably, the family's dog would trot alongside his master, sniffing merrily along the way.

Today the picture hasn't changed much. Whether we take a trip by Conestoga wagon or station wagon, there are times when we do want to take along our dog. And unless we get very primitive about our traveling, chances are we won't stop and camp by the roadside when it's time to eat. Therefore, if you are going on a motor trip,

A short vacation jaunt

whether it be a hunting and fishing trip or just a short vacation jaunt, and you plan to take your dog, you should make some careful preparations for feeding him.

First of all, don't let your dog eat or drink for a few hours before you even start backing out of the driveway. Dogs have a tendency to get travel sick, and until they get used to the motion of the ve-

Don't let your dog eat or drink for a few hours

An auto trip is a very exciting event in his life

hicle, they shouldn't have anything to eat or drink. If you'd like to ensure against further travel sickness, you may want to give your dog a tranquilizer, like Dramamine, with the advice of your veterinarian, of course.

Have you ever noticed that at dog shows many owners have brought along bottled water for their dogs? Well, some dogs have such sensitive taste that they can't drink any water but home brew! When you travel, you may find this to be true about your dog, so be prepared to take along a bottle of clear, cool water for him.

The most important thing to remember about feeding him while on an automobile trip is that it's a very exciting event in his life. He may get so excited that he forgets his early toilet training. Therefore, the main point in feeding is to suppress his need for defecation. Help him be a little constipated and you will save time and energy cleaning up after him. One way to do this is to feed him lean meat a day or so before you leave. The small residue left by meat enables your dog to go for a long while without defecating. Also, don't feed him highly seasoned foods. Salty and seasoned foods will make him thirsty and will thus soften his stool.

While actually on the road take along canned dog foods, biscuit, and kibble. Canned foods are perfect, providing you just give him a

While actually on the road
take along canned dog foods, biscuit, and kibble

small amount, since the water content in the food may increase his desire for urination and defecation.

Always make sure that you either take along his own bowl or paper plates, which are easily disposable and, obviously, don't need washing. And, if you stop at a hotel or motel overnight, you won't be able to take your dog into the dining room with you (unless you want to be asked to leave before check-out time), so make sure that he eats before or after you do, but not with you! You can probably feed him right in your room out of his bowl without angering the management. If they let you bring him along in the first place, they won't mind him eating, providing you don't let him get too sloppy.

Next time you take a motor trip and have the family jalopy packed up to the roof, as you're putting on the last suitcase, don't be afraid to put on the dog, if you so desire. With a little common sense you should have no trouble in your travels. Have fun!

10
Senior Citizens

The twilight years

Come out from behind that newspaper! Just because your dog is a senior citizen, that's no reason to ignore him. As a matter of fact, now is the time when you should be a little more tolerant. After all, he's served you well all these years!

Part of being tolerant of his geriatric whims is making a little adjustment in his dinner fare. There are a few simple rules you can follow which will make the last few years of his life a pleasant interlude between the joys of a youthful, vigorous life and that fireplug-lined dog Valhalla in the sky.

The most important thing to remember about an old dog as he enters the twilight years is that he now leads a less strenuous life. He's quite content with standing guard in front of the refrigerator for hours on end just to make sure it's still there when mealtime rolls around.

Just like the rules for human food consumption during old age, common sense dictates that the lack of a strenuous, active life for a dog means a cutting down in the amount of food he eats. You see, this is the time of life when you should be extra-careful that your dog doesn't put on any surplus weight. Fat may accumulate around his heart, just as it does with humans, and shorten his life considerably. In short, fellow dog lovers, remember that, no matter how long your dog camps in front of that refrigerated storehouse of temptation, he is to get less food at dinner than he enjoyed in the most active of his salad days.

If he does get fat, don't put him on a "crash" diet. You may, in fact, increase the number of meals he gets, but just cut down on the amount of food in each meal. And no snacks between meals. Those hearty gulps between meals mean added weight. A strong reason for increasing the number of meals the geriatric dog gets is that, as he gets older, he may not get the full benefit from food that is served in large amounts. Therefore, either he gets a vitamin prescription from your veterinarian, or you may want to increase the number of meals, while decreasing the amount in each.

Your old dog is liable to have a finicky appetite now that he's a member of the Golden Age Club. Therefore, he may not bound excitedly to his bowl any more when the dinner gong sounds. What's the remedy? Well, play up to his nose. He may have lost his vigor,

Guarding the refrigerator for hours on end

Let the hearty aroma of a good, home-cooked meal
waft its way into his nostrils . . .

but he certainly hasn't lost his olfactory senses. If you let the hearty aroma of a good, home-cooked meal waft its way into his nostrils, you may help restore his interest in food. And a hearty aroma will also help a great deal in starting his digestive juices flowing. Feed him soup and he will be bluffed into eating even though he doesn't want to (see Chapter 3, "Soup's On!").

The best food you can give your old dog is, of course, meat. Meat aids in repair of damaged tissue and keeps him from putting on those nasty pounds. Also, make sure that he gets his vitamins and minerals in the vegetables he eats. This will aid in building his resistance to these old-age illnesses.

Here are a few tips in feeding the Methuselah set: You can help prevent tartar from forming on an old dog's teeth by letting him chew on dog biscuits. Some dog owners let their dog chew on a piece of knotted rawhide, which can be purchased inexpensively at your pet shop. The rawhide has a strong smell, which a dog loves, and he'll chew away quite contentedly without increasing his caloric intake.

Old dogs tend to be constipated. Make sure that an old dog gets his regular exercise (but not too many push-ups, please). Exercise

Old dogs tend to be constipated

The teatime of life
Inspired by Sir William Nicholson's famous engraving of Queen Victoria

will help encourage elimination, and since he has reached retirement age, don't let him overdo it. If he has chronic constipation, give him a laxative, like milk of magnesia or any other laxatives your veterinarian may recommend.

With these few simple rules in mind, and the valuable information your veterinarian will be glad to give you, here's hoping you make your dog's last few years on earth a pleasure-filled experience. He deserves it!

TV DINNER

½ pound lamb, with bone
Kibble
Milk
2 dog biscuits

Cut up meat into chunks. Include bone. Mix kibble with lamb. Moisten with milk. Serve in bowl. Serve biscuits for dessert!

BOXER'S BRUNCH

2 eggs
4 strips bacon
Milk
Dog biscuits

Soft-boil eggs (4 minutes). Cook bacon. Break up bacon into bits and add to eggs. Add some warm milk and biscuits. Serve warm.

MEAT AND TOMATO

Leftover meat
1 can tomato soup, undiluted
Milk
Dog biscuits
Grated cheese

Add meat to soup and heat. Add some milk while still heating. Mix in dog biscuits, sprinkle with grated cheese, and serve warm.

HEART CHEWIES

½ pound beef hearts
Leftover vegetables
Soda crackers
Bacon, lamb, or chicken fat

Cut up beef hearts and place in dog bowl. Add warmed leftover vegetables and crumbled soda crackers. Pour fat over mixture. Serve.

CANINE CRUMBLE*

¼ pound chopped meat
1 small onion, chopped
½ green pepper, chopped
1 tablespoon flour
1 can vegetable soup, undiluted
Milk
Grated cheese

Sauté meat, onion, pepper. Sprinkle in flour. Add soup and some milk. Cook until warm (about 10 minutes). Serve warm topped with cheese.

NEW ENGLAND DELIGHT

Leftover meat
1 can cream of mushroom soup, undiluted
1 egg
Oyster crackers
Grated cheese

Cut up meat into chunks and add to soup. Warm mixture. Add soft-boiled egg (4 minutes). Add handful of oyster crackers and top with grated cheese. Serve warm.

ST. PATTY'S SPECIAL

¼ pound chopped meat
Prepared wheat biscuit
1 can split-pea soup, undiluted

Sauté meat. Mix in a couple of squares of shredded wheat, add warmed soup. Serve warm.

MUSHROOM CLOUD

1 can dog food
½ can cream of mushroom soup, undiluted
Handful of kibble

Thoroughly mix dog food with warmed mushroom soup. Add kibble. Serve.

DRY DINNER

To a bowl of dry dog meal add either leftover meat chunks or raw chopped meat. Pour warmed chicken, bacon, or lamb fat over mixture. Add enough crumbled soda crackers to absorb moisture. Serve.

CHICKEN AND TOMATO SMASH

Leftover chicken
½ can stewed tomatoes, drained
Cottage cheese
Kibble

Warm chicken and tomatoes. Mix in cottage cheese and kibble. Serve.

11

Rewards and Special Treats

Fix him something special . . .

Do you feel as if you should feed your dog something special? Well, you should! After all, *he's* special. He's been a first-class citizen—a real friend—and he deserves a little special delicacy on occasion. Now, I'm not advocating that he get a gourmet's delight every day, but there are times when you may want to titillate his taste buds with a tasty treat.

When do you give him a special tidbit? After his bath is a good time. Or just after grooming him, or when he learns a new trick. His birthday is a festive occasion, and you may want to reward him then. Or, if you are going on a trip, and your dog is a little excited, you may reward him with a goody to calm him down for the day's activities. Remember, a tempting reward at the right occasion will make him love you more than he already does.

Every dog has his own favorite reward or special treat, but there are some that have become universal in dogdom. And here they are:

After his bath is a good time . . .

Chicken giblets make an especially fine treat. Or you may want to boil the backs and necks (make sure that there are no bones included), adding vegetables and noodles, to make a little stewy treat for him.

One Park Avenue dog owner I know (she has a toy poodle named Fifi) makes *arroz con pollo* for her pet once a week. Fifi discovered this delectable dish while on an excursion to Mexico, and she's loved it ever since.

His birthday is a festive occasion . . .

Eggs can make a very simple special treat for your dog. Make sure that they're cooked, not raw. Egg white that is uncooked destroys biotin, an essential vitamin, in his intestine; some veterinarians feel that dogs should not have raw egg white. You may want to ask your own doctor about this. The yolk may be served raw, though. When you cook eggs, hard-cook or soft-boil them. If you hard-cook them, you may want to let your dog eat them shells and all. One dog owner I know does this with regularity, claiming that the shells provide an excellent source of calcium for her boxers. One variation in egg treats for dogs is practiced by a former short-order cook I know, who feeds his dog bacon and eggs for Sunday brunch as a special treat.

And, just as elegant a reward for our canine friends is the special treat a New Jersey boxer takes great delight in. Bonnie, the boxer, just loves to sit and watch boxing matches on television munching on a ham and cheese sandwich with a saucer of beer by her side. Naturally, just like Pavlov's pets, every time the gong rings for the next round, she begins to munch away voraciously!

Of course, some of these special treats can get too extreme. If you want to go to great lengths to prepare special delights for your dog, there's no one stopping you, but, in general, a simple delight such as a handful of dog biscuits or a piece of candy will suffice. Usually

Beer, sandwiches, and the fights on TV

A simple delight will suffice . . .

dogs will be perfectly happy with a few biscuits or candy or ice cream.

And, a word about the subject of ice cream and candy! Most dog owners will agree that ice cream and candy in large amounts can be detrimental to their pets. But on great occasions (birthdays, births, etc.) a small serving of ice cream or a piece of candy or lump of sugar may be just the right reward for your dog (see Chapter 6, "Pregnant Paws").

Actually, the best reward your dog can get is a kind word and a hearty pat on the head, but of course, food fool that he is, a smidgen of his favorite food will send him into an orgy of renewed devotion. So, break out the baked Alaska, boys and girls, you may as well be prepared!

12
Helpful Hints

Here are some hints and short cuts you may find helpful toward planning your dog's dinners:

1. If and when your dog eats canned food, and you find that the smell of it, although perfectly acceptable to him, leaves you gasping for air, you can eliminate the offensive odor by keeping the can in the refrigerator before opening it. Also, between servings, if there is some left over, refrigerate the contents. This way you won't notice the odor, and your dog won't notice the difference. When you do serve the chilled food, mix it with a little warm water. The water will ensure that the food isn't too cold.

2. Crumble a little charcoal into powder or small lumps and add it to your dog's dinner once a week. The charcoal absorbs the gas in his stomach, helps relieve indigestion, and will help correct diarrhea. The charcoal is not digested by your dog, but is naturally eliminated in the due course of events. Many of the prepared dry dog foods have charcoal included in them, so that if you use a prepared dinner, read the ingredients, and if there is charcoal included, this will be sufficient for him.

3. If your dog is constipated, liver is a good laxative.

4. If your dog won't drink milk, or if you want to take some milk for him while you are on a trip, use powdered milk. Just add a little

The book-review section makes an ideal place mat

to his dinner. The powder will be absorbed into the food, or will turn into skim milk when it comes in contact with the water in his dinner. He will get all the essential elements of milk quickly, easily, and painlessly. Powdered milk is especially good for old dogs and summertime feeding, since there is little or no fat content.

5. If you have a nervous dog, or one who gets upset when company comes and vomits his dinner in the excitement, try feeding him late at night at an hour when there's little chance of a visit to disturb his peace and tranquillity.

6. Aluminum feeding pans or crockery bowls are the best dishes for feeding your dog. Why? They are easy to keep clean. Make sure you use a dish that is wider at the base than at the rim. This will prevent him from tipping it over in his hurry to get dinner.

If you have a flexible schedule, make sure that your dog has one too

If your dog won't eat his dinner, don't force him

7. If you have a large dog who is sloppy in his eating habits, here's a tip that will save your bending over and cleaning up after every meal. The book review section of the Sunday newspaper makes an excellent tablecloth! It has the right number of pages and is the right size to make a protective shield between his jaws and your floor.

8. A good time to feed your dog, generally, is in the morning when you are having breakfast. There is always someone home for breakfast, and thus your dog is assured of having his meal.

9. When your dog whimpers for food, don't feed him. Wait until he has stopped. If you give in to his whim and whimper, he will soon learn that he can get his way with just a little academic whining.

10. You may want to vary your dog's mealtime a little each day (maybe a half-hour variation) so that he doesn't get accustomed to a fixed routine. This way, if you happen to sleep late on Sunday, he won't be pulling at your covers for breakfast! If you have a flexible schedule, make sure that your dog has one too. Don't let him regulate your schedule; he must learn to live by your set of regulations.

11. Your dog will be healthier and happier if you feed him small portions of the proper food rather than large quantities. Also, he will be better off not eating too many table scraps. He can eat some scraps, but the main portion of his diet should be well balanced.

Each dog has his own peculiarities

12. Your dog should be slightly hungry at the end of a meal, rather than overfed. If he is overfed all the time, he can become sluggish and fat, which can be detrimental to his health.

13. Don't feed your dog from your plate, even if he comes nosing around. He may get accustomed to begging, and he certainly won't develop good eating habits.

14. If your dog is tempted to run off, and sharp verbal commands won't bring him back to the home and hearth, you may, on occasion, want to offer him some of his favorite foods as a lure.

15. If your dog won't eat his dinner, don't force him. He may have learned that by pouting he can trick you into giving him his favorite food rather than what's best for him. Don't let him get away with this! After about fifteen minutes, take his bowl away, and don't feed him again until the next mealtime. He won't starve. When he gets hungry enough to eat, he'll be happy to dive into his bowl full of the foods you've selected for him.

Naturally, you will find (or have found) many hints and short cuts of your own which will be a great help in the kitchen. Each dog has his own peculiarities and habits, and these may alter the short cuts you adopt regarding his care. The few hints I have mentioned seem to be somewhat universal in their appeal, while they are general enough to be applied to any dog. Keep on searching!